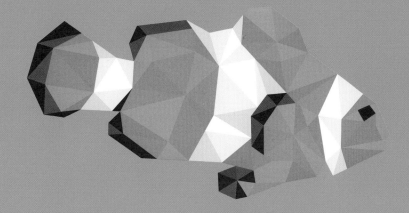

My Sticker Paintings
OCEAN ANIMALS

DOLPHIN
INTERMEDIATE

OCTOPUS
INTERMEDIATE

ORCA (KILLER WHALE)
EASY

CRAB
EASY

SEAHORSE
HARD

MANTA RAY
EASY

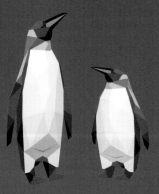

JELLYFISH
HARD

**EMPEROR
PENGUIN**
INTERMEDIATE

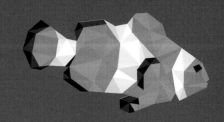

CLOWNFISH
HARD

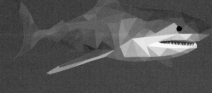

GREAT WHITE SHARK
EASY

DOLPHIN

DOLPHIN

KEY FACTS

FAMILY: mammals

BABY NAME: calf

SIZE: 5.5 to 8 feet

WEIGHT: 150 to 240 pounds

HABITAT: oceans and seas

DIET: small fish (herring, sardines), mollusks, and crustaceans

LIFE SPAN: 30 to 50 years

Did you know?

Dolphins emit ultrasonic sounds that allow them to detect different objects: the sound waves hit obstacles and bounce back as echoes.

These excellent swimmers wander the oceans to follow schools of fish. Their curved fins and flippers allow them to move and turn around in the water. Their tail fin helps propel them and even allows them to leap out of the water. They live in groups called pods and communicate using whistles.

OCTOPUS

OCTOPUS

Did you know?

Octopuses are the ultimate copycats; they are capable of imitating the texture and color of other animals, plants, and rocks.

Octopuses do not have a skeleton but have eight tentacles that can grow back if they are lost. These are covered in hundreds of suckers that allow the octopus to capture its prey, sense it, and taste it; the suckers also allow the octopus to grip and move. To escape their predators, octopuses can release clouds of ink.

SEAHORSE

SEAHORSE

KEY FACTS

FAMILY: fish

SIZE: 1 to 14 inches

WEIGHT: 1.5 to 2.5 ounces

HABITAT: sandy or rocky seabeds, warm and temperate seas

DIET: larvae, plankton, and small fish

LIFE SPAN: 2 to 4 years

Did you know?

The female lays her eggs in the pouch on the male's stomach. He incubates them until they hatch and then takes care of the babies.

With its head and tail that make it look like a horse, the seahorse is a truly funny little fish. Its body is covered in thick bony plates, similar to that of insects. It swims in an upright position, flapping its tiny dorsal fin to propel itself. To rest, it grips onto seaweed or coral with its tail.

CRAB

CRAB

FAMILY: crustaceans

SIZE: 2 to 10 inches

WEIGHT: up to 11 pounds

HABITAT: seabeds and estuaries

DIET: small crustaceans, mollusks, fish, worms, eggs

LIFE SPAN: 10 to 15 years

Did you know?

A crab's gills allow it to absorb oxygen from the water as well as breathe the air. Sometimes, a crab will dig a hole in the sand to hide.

Crabs get around on the sand by walking sideways and backward. They live in the water as well as on beaches at low tide. A crab's soft body is protected by a shell that grows along with the crab. Its two pincers aren't the same size—one is used to catch food and the other to crush the food.

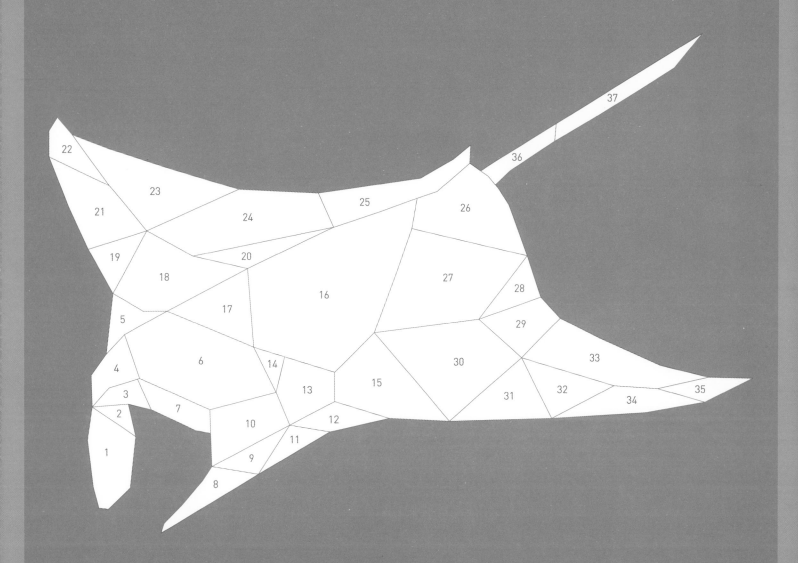

MANTA RAY

MANTA RAY

KEY FACTS

FAMILY: fish

SIZE: 10 to 20 foot wingspan

WEIGHT: 1 to 1.5 tons

HABITAT: warm seas and certain temperate seas, coral reefs

DIET: plankton, small fish, crustaceans, and mollusks

LIFE SPAN: 15 to 20 years

Did you know?

Manta rays leap and glide above the water both to communicate with other rays and to get rid of pesky parasites.

The manta ray, the biggest of all the rays, is recognizable by its large, triangular fins that look like two big wings. It swims by flapping its fins up and down as if it were flying. The two small fins on its head allow it to funnel water into its mouth, helping it eat.

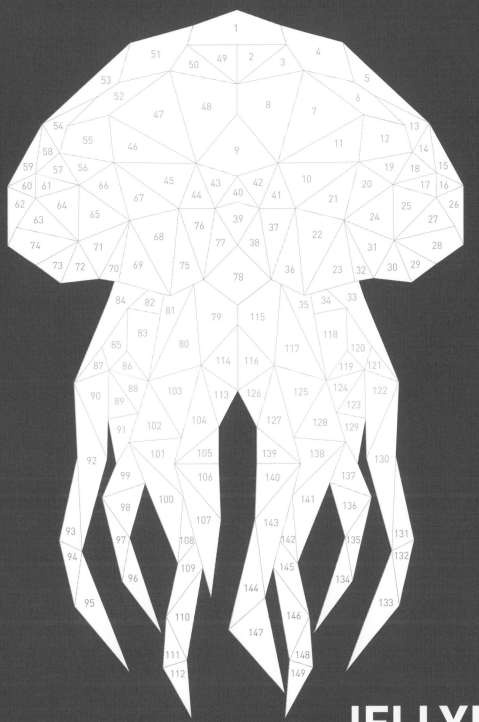

JELLYFISH

JELLYFISH

KEY FACTS

FAMILY: cnidarians

SIZE: 6 to 16 inches in diameter

WEIGHT: 2 to 22 pounds, about 98% water

HABITAT: all oceans

DIET: plankton, small fish, and crustaceans

LIFE SPAN: 2 to 12 months

Did you know?

Jellyfish are known for their sting, but not all jellyfish actually sting or are poisonous. Even so, never touch a jellyfish, because the types that sting can do so whether they are living or not!

Jellyfish have soft bodies made up of an umbrella-shaped bell and venomous tentacles that allow them to capture prey. These tentacles can be up to 130 feet long! Jellyfish don't have brains, hearts, or eyes, and they get around by contracting their bells to propel themselves through the water.

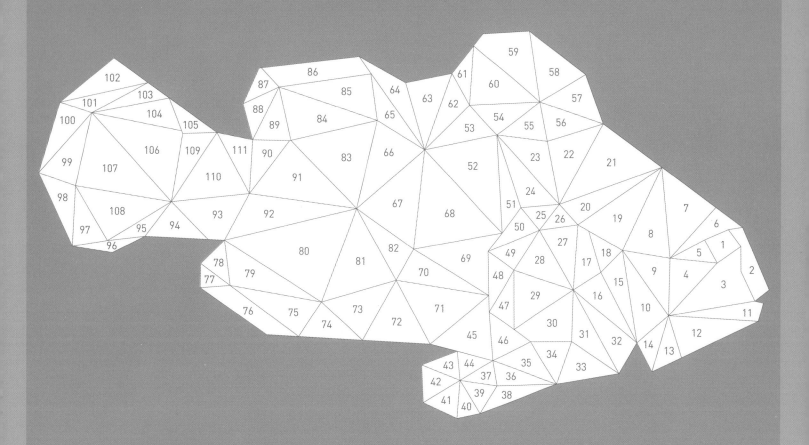

CLOWNFISH

CLOWNFISH

FAMILY: fish

SIZE: 3 to 4 inches

WEIGHT: 3.5 to 5.5 ounces

HABITAT: lagoons and coral reefs

DIET: plankton and small crustaceans

LIFE SPAN: 6 to 10 years

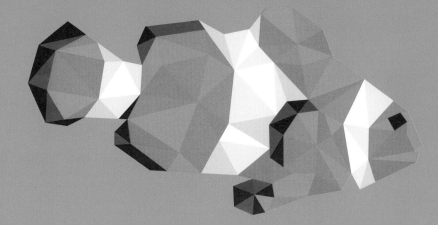

Did you know?

From the moment they are born and as they grow up, baby clownfish get coated in the mucus of the anemones where they live. This coating protects them from the anemones' venom.

Clownfish live in mated pairs inside sea anemones; they don't go farther than 4 inches away from their home. The anemone gives the fish protection from predators with its venomous tentacles. In exchange, the fish get rid of the anemone's parasites and attack the butterflyfish that try to eat the anemone.

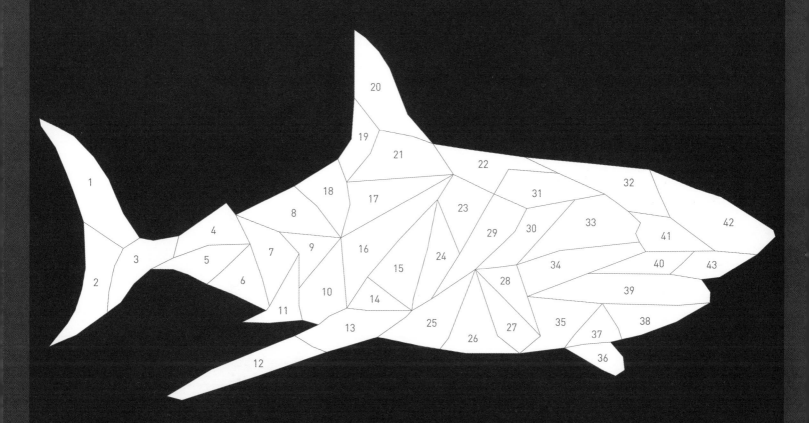

GREAT WHITE SHARK

GREAT WHITE SHARK

Did you know?

There are more than 450 species of sharks. Only 5 are considered dangerous to humans.

The shark is the biggest of all the fish. Thanks to its slender body and powerful muscles, it can swim faster than 25 miles per hour. Its great senses of smell and hearing allow it to detect prey from very far away. Whenever it loses a tooth, another tooth grows in its place!

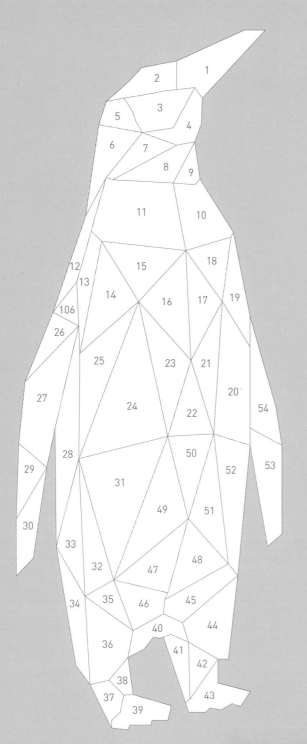
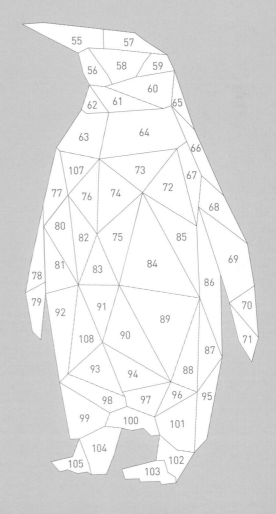

EMPEROR PENGUIN

EMPEROR PENGUIN

FAMILY: marine birds

BABY NAME: chick

SIZE: 3.5 to 4.5 feet

WEIGHT: 44 to 88 pounds

HABITAT: Antarctic ice

DIET: fish, mollusks, and small crustaceans

LIFE SPAN: 15 to 20 years

Did you know?

Penguins all have unique cries, which allow parents to recognize their own chicks within the colony.

A penguin's small wings can't be used to fly, but they are great for swimming! Penguins live in colonies of thousands of individuals. Both parents take turns incubating their single egg, passing the egg from one parent's feet to the other parent's feet so that the egg doesn't freeze by touching the ice.

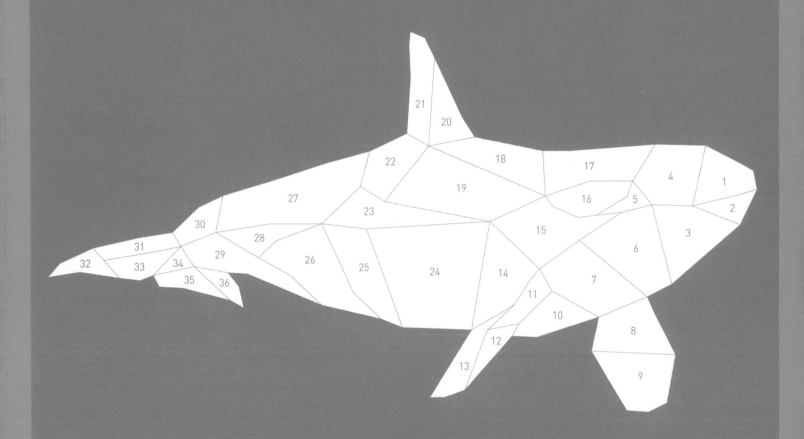

ORCA
(KILLER WHALE)

ORCA
(KILLER WHALE)

FAMILY: mammals

BABY NAME: calf

SIZE: 16.5 to 26 feet long

WEIGHT: 4 to 8 tons

HABITAT: cold seas

DIET: octopuses, squid, fish, marine mammals, birds

LIFE SPAN: 40 to 60 years

Did you know?

To catch seals, an orca can slide up onto beaches or ice. With its tail, it can even knock a flying bird from the sky.

A mammal like the dolphin, the orca is a super predator, which has given it the nickname "killer whale." Orcas usually hunt in groups of around 30 individuals that communicate with each other using ultrasound. When an orca is swimming, its colors blend easily with the water, making it seem invisible.

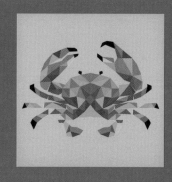

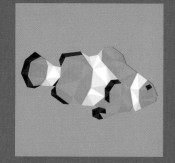

STICKERS

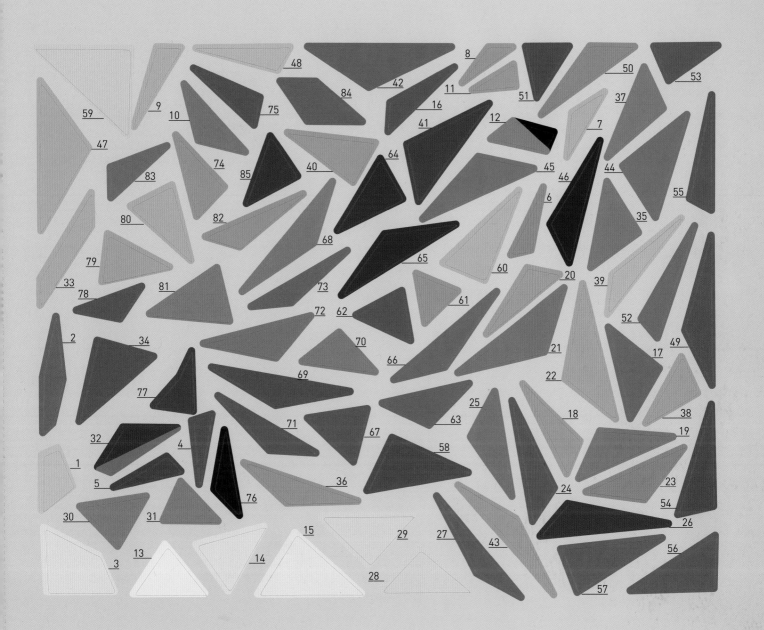

DOLPHIN

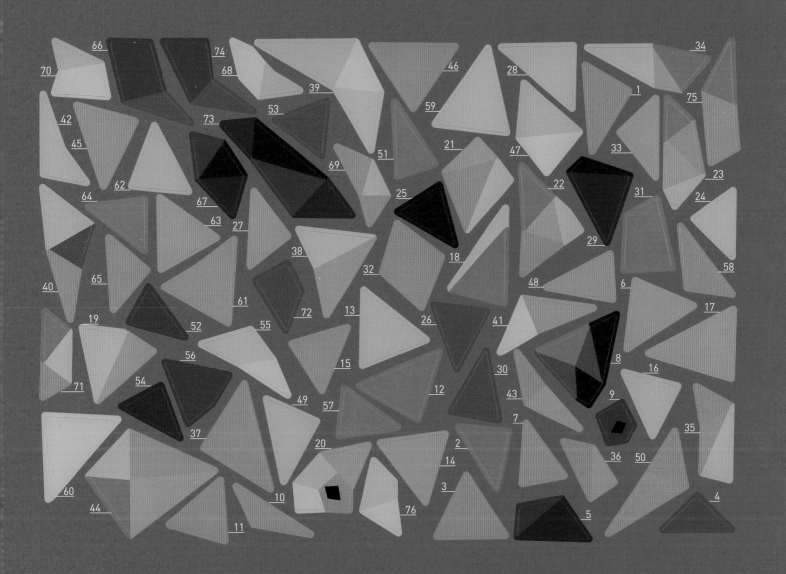

OCTOPUS

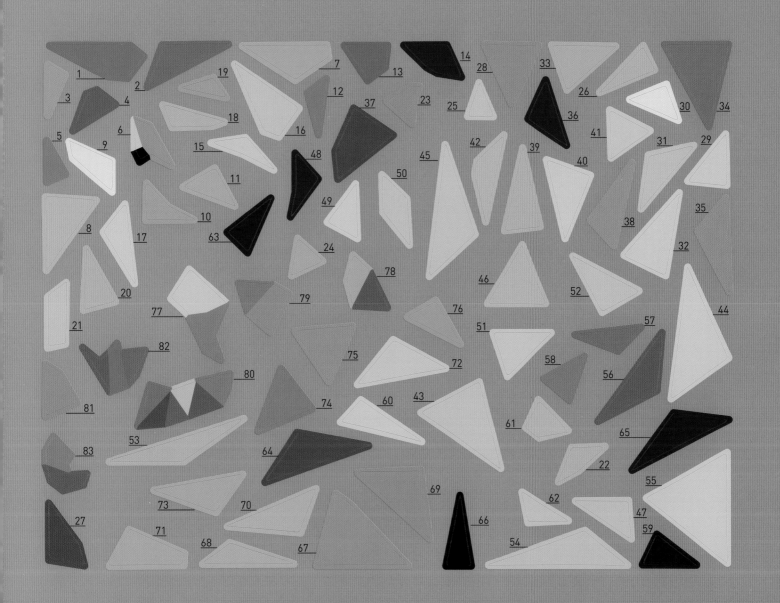

SEAHORSE

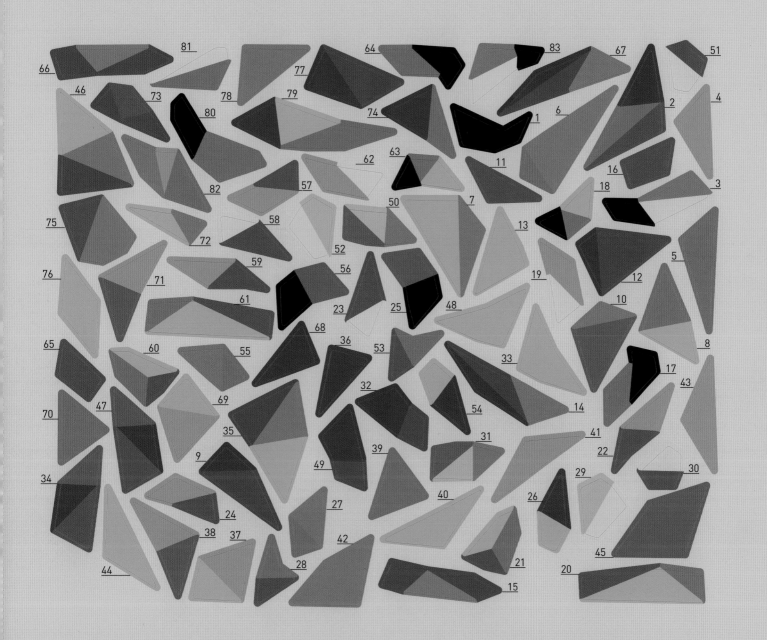

CRAB

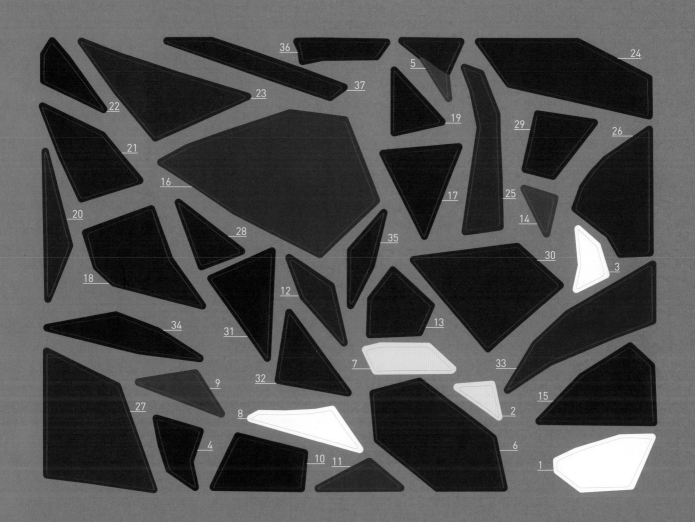

MANTA RAY

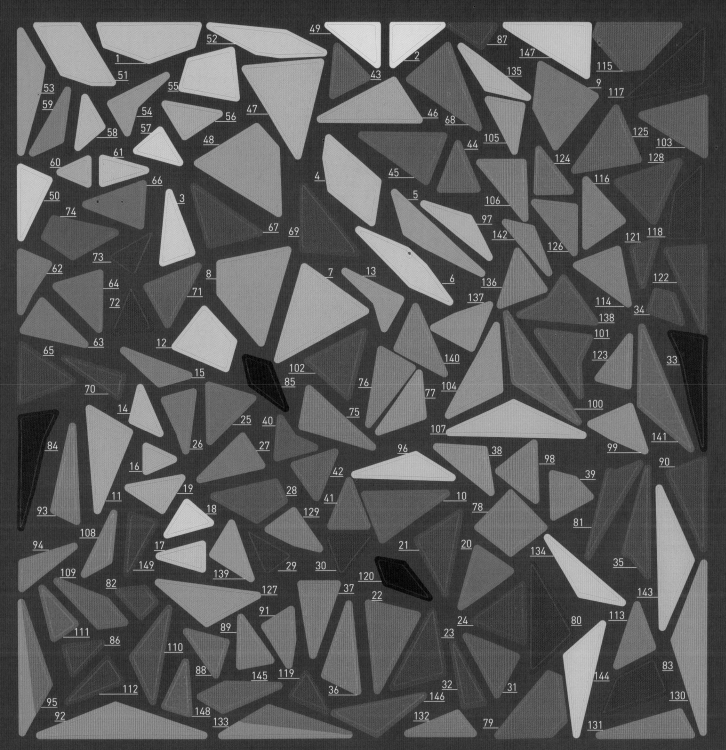

JELLYFISH

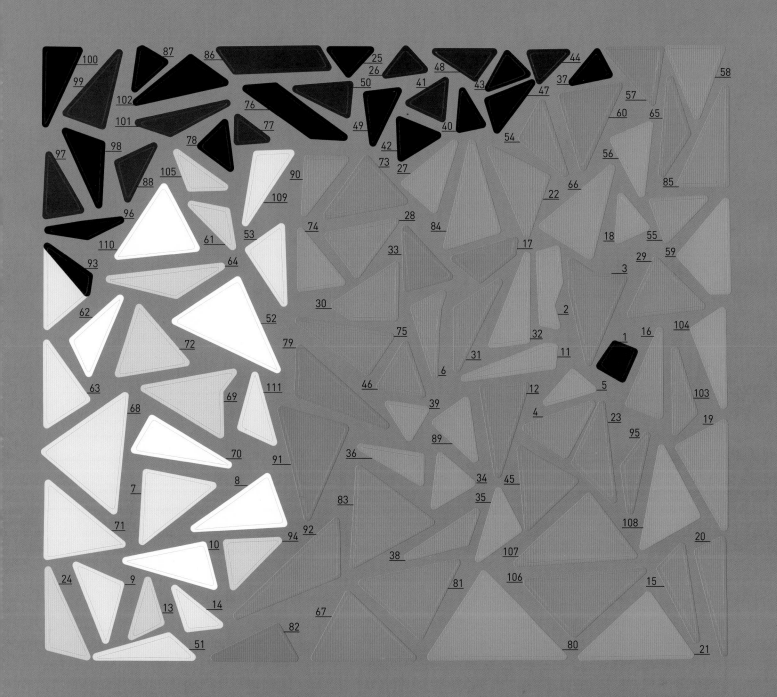

CLOWNFISH

GREAT WHITE SHARK

EMPEROR PENGUIN

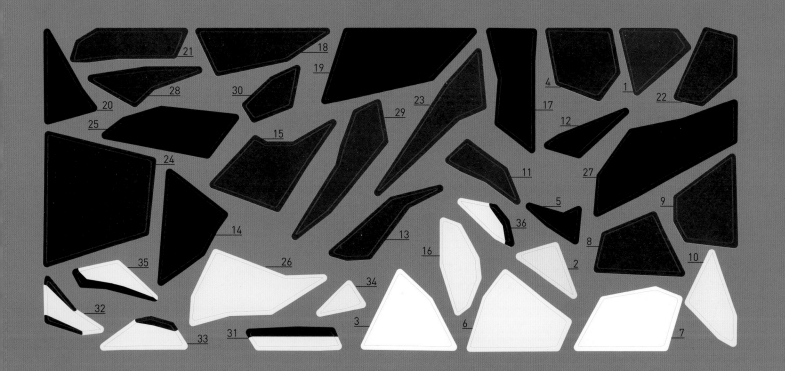

ORCA
(KILLER WHALE)